THE CONSTRUCT LESSON PLAN
Improving Group Instruction

The Instructional Design Library

Volume 7

THE CONSTRUCT LESSON PLAN
Improving Group Instruction

Danny G. Langdon

Director of Instructional Design Research
The American College
Bryn Mawr, Pennsylvania

Danny G. Langdon
Series Editor

Educational Technology Publications
Englewood Cliffs, New Jersey 07632

Library of Congress Cataloging in Publication Data

Langdon, Danny G
    The construct lesson plan.

    (The Instructional design library; v. no. 7)
    Bibliography: p.
    1. Lesson planning. 2 Home and school. I. Title.
II. Series.
LB1027.L248   371.3   77-25406
ISBN 0-87778-111-7

Printed in the United States of America.

Library of Congress Catalog Card Number: 77-25406.

International Standard Book Number: 0-87778-111-7.

First Printing: February, 1978.

PREFACE

This is my baby. I've had a great deal of personal satisfaction and sense of having contributed to effective learning with this instructional design. The Construct Lesson Plan approach *works* for both students and teachers.

Certainly, I would not claim this design to be the final answer to classroom instruction, but it is a solid foundation for adding other needs while one is trying to assure a basic level of effective and efficient group instruction.

There are so many people to thank in regard to this design that I can't possibly list them all. There are a few hundred students, a score and more of teachers, many professional colleagues, some very competent research evaluators, several subject matter experts, and many·typists. This amounts to about five years worth of work and excitement. I especially want to thank The American College for its generous support in allowing me to pursue an idea to its fullest extent.

D.G.L.

CONTENTS

ABSTRACT

THE CONSTRUCT LESSON PLAN

Designed to be used in a group, classroom situation which is led by a teacher, this instructional design aims to assist the teacher in achieving instructional efficiency and effectiveness.

Efficiency in classroom instruction can be greatly improved by specifically accounting for objectives students learn on their own as a result, primarily, of assigned preparatory study. The teacher accounts for objectives the students have learned on their own (through diagnostic, self-testing means), and *constructs* or assembles a lesson plan based on such an analysis. The *lesson plan* is constructed to the immediate learning needs (objectives) of the students as a group, and is implemented by whatever means the teacher may wish —lecture, discussion, project, discovery, etc. *Lesson Plan Cards* and a *Content Outline* are the basic instructional components used by the teacher, while the students use a *Pretest* to indicate their mastery of objectives upon entering the classroom.

One additional and particularly noteworthy aspect of this instructional design is that it includes, as a built-in feature of implementation, its own validation instrument for judging the effectiveness of classroom instruction. Upon this validation, decisions can be made to further improve classroom instruction.

THE CONSTRUCT LESSON PLAN
Improving Group Instruction

I.

USE

When one thinks about it, most classroom instruction is inefficient. Say this statement in some faculty rooms, and you may be courting a debate. But far from a statement meant to *turn a teacher off*, it is made to gain recognition for the topic: *Why is classroom instruction basically inefficient, and what can we do about inefficiency?* Classroom instruction often takes up a great deal of valuable time by focusing on concepts and skills that students *could have learned already* through assigned preparatory study, or by reviewing skills and concepts that students have already mastered as part of their general background knowledge. Inefficiency, as referred to here, should *not* be misinterpreted to mean that classroom instruction is unnecessary; or that in many instances it does not contain a great deal of effectiveness (student learning) and efficiency (student time and effort in learning). It is just that, generally, teachers assign much preparatory work to students, and then end up rehashing much of what was learned in the preparatory study. This waste of time is then rationalized away, and teachers go along with the practice of covering things again. This is partly because, as teachers, we prepare each day for a complete lesson, and therefore deliver and guide a complete lesson. But, it is also because we are not necessarily aware of inefficiency and the means by which it can be overcome.

3

Put in the form of another rationalization, it is sometimes said that the task of the teacher is to put what the students have read into *perspective* in order to make sure the students have learned. Whatever rationalization is used, it comes out as a waste of time.

If we are honest with ourselves, if we accept the premise that students *do* learn something prior to entering the classroom and that our task is not to rehash it, then we should investigate how to make our in-class instruction more efficient. Specifically, the achievement of efficiency referred to is that of directing our in-class instructional time to *those learning objectives with which the students really need help*, and not to those that they have already learned by themselves. The Construct Lesson Plan instructional design is one such means of assuring a higher degree of in-class efficiency of instruction. It is not the only way, and different approaches have been suggested by others, such as individualized, self-paced, and student-controlled designs. But these are approaches for *individuals*: and, if the intent is to provide *group/classroom* instruction, or a teacher is just stuck with it—in the classical sense of a teacher providing and guiding the instruction of a group of students—then we are back to the kind of instructional design that can be used by a teacher. That is where the Construct Lesson Plan will find its principal use.

The use of a Construct Lesson Plan is for *classroom, group instruction*. However, it is *an attempt to individualize learning in the classroom environment*. It is presupposed that such group instruction is preceded by preparatory study on the part of the students, possibly through use of one of the other instructional designs suggested in the Instructional Design Library (e.g., Adjunct Study Guide) or at least some other form of outside preparatory study (such as the more traditional reading assignments from a textbook).

The emphasis given thus far to the use of the Construct Lesson Plan has been that of dealing with learning efficiency. However, this is not the only problem of classroom instruction which it addresses.

In part, because the title of this instructional design is *lesson plan,* it implies a teacher's prescription of student learning events. But what the title doesn't connote directly is the role of the student in helping to decide exactly what the lesson will be. For the moment, let us understand what is meant by *lesson plan.*

Every teacher has a lesson plan of one kind or another. Many carry these plans around in their heads or use an existing text as a guide to their lessons. Still others have a written set of notes, which is the kind of thing we usually think of as being a lesson plan.

Lesson plans exist to serve two primary functions. First, they are plans of what will occur in the classroom. In this sense, a lesson plan is a kind of reminder pad for critical content, activities, media to be used, exercises, and so forth. They are not, however, scripts to be read.

The second, and least utilized, function of a lesson plan is for recording necessary changes which will make the lesson effective for future use. In other words, the repeated use of a lesson with groups of students may show signs of apparent weaknesses in instruction, and we can formulate new activities, exercises, content sequences, examples, or find new media to help overcome these weaknesses. The results of periodic achievement tests also should indicate needed changes to be made in the lesson plan. If no written lesson plan exists, then there is no place, other than in our heads, for recording these changes for future use.

The need for a written lesson plan is apparent, for two major reasons. It is a reminder of what is to happen; and it is a source upon which to record needed changes for future use. Still, there are additional reasons why a written lesson plan is needed.

Group-oriented instruction often suffers from a lack of continuity from one class setting to the next. Even the most experienced teacher has been aware that his or her presentation varies in *quality* from class to class. The problem of quality, as with other problems associated with group instruction, is even more apparent when viewed from the standpoint of the students.

For one thing, students generally experience difficulty ascertaining the *critical content* of a lesson plan presentation. Even the task of taking notes goes far beyond desirable limits, so that some content is totally missed and other content is recorded incorrectly. Furthermore, related to this attempt to acquire and record the content is a general lack of continuous responding that allows a student to assess his or her own progress. Also missing is feedback which tells the student he or she responded correctly or incorrectly. The general lack of both relevant responses and feedback is not only a student problem in terms of assessing learning progress, but it is also a teacher problem. The lack of active responding and feedback means the teacher has difficulty assessing individual and group progress during instruction and adapting to it quickly when progress is not being achieved.

In general, a lesson plan does attempt to deal with the problem of continuity in instruction. There is usually a content outline, examples and practice exercises in a sequence for the teacher to remember for presentation. The student problems associated with *identifying critical content, active responding,* and *feedback* are the components most often overlooked in the usual lesson plan. An interactive lesson plan, on the other hand, such as the one suggested here, will overcome these problems.

A lesson plan is mainly teacher oriented. It is important, therefore, that the prescription of instruction within the lesson plan be stringent in prescribing what must occur; yet it must be flexible, so that interaction can take place.

A *canned* interactive instructional design, such as a film or audio recording, will be presented the same way every time. Compare this to a teacher presentation via a lesson plan wherein each lesson is not presented the same way every time. In the teacher lesson plan, there exists a double-edged sword of flexibility—the highly desirable capability of the teacher to adapt to student learning needs, with a flexibility that mistakenly might not provide students with all the interaction and content they need to achieve course objectives.

As noted earlier, a lesson plan is not simply a script to be read by a teacher. It is a sequence of topics to be discussed— but always aimed at the objectives to be achieved by the students. At appropriate points, the teacher asks questions to provide students with the opportunity to assess their own learning and to provide feedback to the teacher on individual and group progress.

Finally, there is one use of the Construct Lesson Plan which has barely been touched upon. This is its use to improve on the efficiency of classroom instruction. Efficiency is important and rarely thought of when designing or implementing instruction. Like effectiveness, which is how well students learn, efficiency has some relationship to such concerns as maintaining student interest and avoiding problems related to student boredom. Efficiency has, of course, a direct relationship to the dollars and cents of instruction.

Efficiency of instruction will be improved because the Construct Lesson Plan approach allows the teacher to account for what students learn on their own; and, therefore, the teacher can concentrate instruction on the areas in which students need help. In theory at least, the CLP approach says that if students come to class and have already learned on their own what the teacher had planned for a lesson, then the students could be excused from that lesson. As a practical matter, schools are generally not prepared to deal with such a set of circumstances, although it might be practical in *industrial schoolhouses*. Nonetheless, if such should happen in the usual school classroom, there is then additional time available for dealing with individual student learning needs.

As to the range of potential application of the CLP approach to subject areas and level of instruction, the range of possibilities is enormous. Generally, the CLP approach could be used when and wherever preparatory study is or could be expected of students. Therefore, some limitations probably exist at the lower levels of education, say the third grade and below, where preparatory study is not usually expected or possibly needed. More typical applications are bound to present themselves at the secondary education level and up. Adult education programs, in particular, will find the CLP approach useful.

The applications in subject areas would include most courses, since most are subject matter content oriented. There is a limitation in regard to courses which would be primarily psychomotor (manipulative skills) oriented. However, even in these courses, there is much background information of a *content* nature which can be taught by the CLP approach. Even in courses which use a highly independent, individualized, self-paced design, the CLP can be used to effectively plan and deliver group instruction as it might be needed—for example, as an integrated part of PSI (Keller Plan) programs.

In summary, then, the Construct Lesson Plan instructional design is a lesson plan approach to group, classroom instruction, designed to improve learning efficiency and effectiveness. Efficiency is achieved by accounting for and following through on what students have learned on their own through preparatory study. Effectiveness is achieved by additional time made available as a result of improved efficiency and the interactive components of the lesson plan for active student responding and feedback. In addition, the CLP has its own evaluation/validation devices built into the implementation approach; these devices aid in showing apparent weaknesses of group instruction, which must then be resolved.

II.

OPERATIONAL DESCRIPTION

The Construct Lesson Plan is a preplanned lesson plan that is *constructed* (assembled) by the teacher, *in the classroom,* prior to beginning instruction itself, and which is designed to meet the current student learning needs as those needs fall due when students enter the classroom. In the following operational description, you will see the definition's full meaning; and, in the next chapter, the *Design Format,* examples will be provided of each instructional component of the CLP.

First, the lesson plan is a preplanned lesson. That is, the teacher prepares the lesson, as one would usually do, in advance of actual use in the classroom. The difference between a CLP and most any other lesson plan is that the CLP is a *potential* lesson plan for implementation. Not all of the preplanned lesson plan will necessarily be used. It is *potential* in that, in actual use in the classroom, only selected parts of the total lesson will probably be used in the detail to which is was preplanned. The part which will be used will be determined by the collection of valid data in the first few minutes of a class session. This data will assess what the students have not learned on their own through preparatory study (which the teacher has assigned them in advance). At this stage of the explanation of the CLP, it is important to grasp the understanding that the lesson will be primarily based on those objectives in which the students need the most help—although the lesson will not totally ignore what the students have already learned, for to do so would cause fragmentation of the total lesson. Although this approach to classroom instruction might equally be divided into a smaller or greater number of steps, the author sees it basically as a six step process:

1. Preplanning
2. Preparatory Study
3. Diagnostic Testing
4. Assessing Test Results
5. Assembling the Lesson Plan
6. Implementation and Feedback

Preplanning

Preplanning, in the general sense, means the formulation of a specific lesson (module, class session, assignment, or other units), including such considerations as learner objectives, content, student activities, media utilization, group projects, and necessary and usually structured forms of interaction which would assess whether learning in the classroom is taking place. All of these preplanning activities and others will be part of a Construct Lesson Plan as well. However, in the CLP, as previously stressed, such preplanning must be structured so that only those pieces which will be needed for meeting immediate learning needs will be selected out of the total preparation for actual use. The layout (format) of the instructional design for the CLP will have to allow for this flexibility to select against need. This will be accomplished by what are termed *lesson plan cards,* to be explained later.

A second major aspect of preplanning is the development of the means by which the teacher will assess what the students have learned on their own. Another way to state this is a means to assess out of the total preplanning effort that which actually will be used in its entirety in the classroom as instruction. Here we will focus on the most valid and easiest to administer means of assessment, which will be labeled the Testing Pattern. This involves the use of a diagnostic pretest which measures all the objectives of a forthcoming, pre-planned lesson. Students will take this pretest after completing their preparatory study and prior to entering the classroom where a lesson is to be conducted on the objectives of a lesson. The test will be completed outside of the classroom, but *scored* in the classroom. More will be said about the nature and use of this test very shortly when describing the third step, diagnostic testing. Before describing the diagnostic test, a few comments are necessary on the second major step in the Construct Lesson Plan approach—Preparatory Study.

Preparatory Study

As part of the total process of making up a lesson plan, the teacher will naturally want to determine what sources the students can use to effectively prepare for a lesson in question. Under the usual circumstances, preparatory study means written textual materials. Obviously, it need not be limited to textbooks, if there is time, money, and availability of other media resources.

Although the CLP will work with any form of preparatory study that can be provided, it is worth noting that the more effective the preparatory study is made, the more time there is going to be for classroom instruction on those (hopefully, few) objectives the students have not learned on their own. Assuming the classroom time made available is used wisely, then learning effectiveness can be improved as well.

Although one of the specific conerns of this book is not the manner in which preparatory study can be provided—

only *that* it be provided—it is suggested that the reader investigate other instructional design formats (e.g., Adjunct Study Guide) within which independent, self-study might be more effectively structured for student use. This is mentioned due to the fact that textbooks are typically noninteractive—that is, lacking necessary interaction and feedback— and consequently not as effective as they could be. At a minimum, the author would recommend at least the provision of a set of learner objectives—the same ones from the teacher's lesson plan—that the student would use along with his or her existing text sources. Specific page references with each objective to the appropriate reading also would be useful.

With preplanning and the provision for preparatory study behind us, we are ready to consider the third step in the CLP approach.

Diagnostic Testing

There are a number of ways in which a teacher might make an assessment of what students know and don't know in regard to learning objectives. Which objectives have the students learned on their own and which will need further attention in the classroom? The ways in which we can make such an assessment include:

1. Using our own experience as teachers, we can identify those objectives with which students in the past have had difficulty. These might also be problem areas for our present students.
2. Ask the current students, as a group, which objectives are presenting problems.
3. The teacher could analyze achievement test results of previous students in terms of performance on specific objectives. It is interesting to note in this regard that normally only the *grades* are retained, rather than student performance as a group on specific objectives.

4. Finally, there can be direct testing of the objectives of a lesson. In the same sense that we test objectives *after* classroom instruction, we could test objectives *prior* to classroom instruction—but after preparatory study—to determine which objectives have been learned by students as a result of the preparatory study. This would mean testing *all* the objectives before classroom instruction, rather than the typical sampling of some of the objectives, as in achievement testing through quizzes and examinations usually done after instruction has occurred.

While all four of these means of assessing student mastery of the objectives of a forthcoming lesson are possible, certain things should be noted regarding the reliability of some of these means, let alone the general consideration as to whether there is enough time available to do any or all of them.

Teacher experience, for instance, while useful as a means of identifying those objectives with which students might need help, is a subjective source. It is impossible to predict if a current group of students will have the same learning difficulties on specific objectives as prior groups of students. This is not to suggest that assessments from experience are not useful, only that they are less reliable than other means that can be used.

Student input, based on the idea that students who have just completed their preparatory study should have a fair idea as to what they have and have not learned on their own, is also subjective. Unless the students were provided some means of self-testing as part of their preparatory study, such that they can self-appraise their own learning progress, it would be difficult for students to tell the teacher what they need help on in the classroom. This would be particularly true when preparatory study was simply in the form of an assignment to read a chapter or two from a typical, noninteractive textbook. There is no self-appraisal in a noninteractive textbook. And, if the students did not have a set of objectives to direct their learning, they might not even be able to tell the teacher specifically what they had learned to a degree that would be usable by the teacher.

We need to find an *objective means* of assessment based on accounting for the performance of students. We can accomplish this in the same manner that we judge performance after instruction—by testing. The only difference is that we are going to do our testing before classroom instruction and to a degree that is *fuller* than we typically do after instruction.

We have come full circle to the meaning and use of diagnostic testing in regard to the CLP approach. Simply put, it is recommended that a test be constructed which will measure all the objectives of a forthcoming lesson (that has been preplanned and for which preparatory study has been assigned and completed by students). Let the students complete this test prior to classroom instruction, and then assess the results for the students as a group. This brings forth a number of questions:

1. Is it possible to do this in the amount of time available for preparatory study and classroom instruction?
2. Will the test really be reliable if the students complete it on their own outside the classroom?
3. How can we *score* the test and still have time available for classroom instruction itself?
4. What kind of test format are we talking about?

Some of the answers to these questions will have to await an inspection of the *Design Format* later, but the answers in order are yes, yes, and I'll show you how for the latter two questions. An important point to remember at this point is that if it is possible and valid to test *after* instruction, as with achievement tests, it should be no less possible and valid to do so *before* instruction with diagnostic tests.

Basically, the nature and form of diagnostic testing to be suggested here for the CLP approach will be a test which is written to measure the mastery of each objective of a forthcoming lesson. If, for example, a lesson is composed of 12 learner objectives, then test items would be written to measure each of these objectives. Most of these test items, for reasons to be explained later, will have to be in the form of multiple-choice items, although a certain amount of completion, short essay, and similar *constructed response* items are possible. Sufficient numbers of test items for each particular objective will have to be written so that the teacher can get a clear and complete assessment of student mastery of a particular objective. The students will complete this test outside the classroom because there is simply not enough time to have them take the test in the classroom, prior to instruction, and still have enough time to conduct instruction. The students take the test after completing all their preparatory study, usually the night before. They bring their completed tests to class. In the first few minutes of the class period, the teacher goes over the results on a group basis to determine what the student group has and has not learned. Why and how this works and why students will cooperate—and indeed how this procedure promotes preparatory study itself—will be discussed later. We will, for now, continue in the description of the three remaining steps to the CLP approach.

What we have in the foregoing description of the operation of the CLP approach is a lesson that has been preplanned; students who have completed their preparatory study; and students who have completed a diagnostic test to measure the learner objectives of the lesson which is about to take place in the classroom. The next step is to assess student group performance on the diagnostic test in the classroom.

Assessing Test Results

Assessing Test Results requires two functions: first, how to assess the students as a group; and, secondly, in a manner that retains confidentiality for the individual student.

Assessment is accomplished through the use of a response device. There are a number of such devices available, ranging from electronic to hand-held cards. Since it is costly and less likely that many classrooms would have electronic devices, it is suggested that the best form of response device is similar to the one shown in Figure 1 (see Appendix for Figure 1 including photographs and instruction on how to construct this device). This wheel responder is inexpensive, portable, and particularly suited for retaining confidentiality. Besides, you can make it yourself and use it for several classes.

The wheel responder shown in Figure 1 is divided on both sides into six pie-shaped areas. On one side—the side which will face the teacher—each pie shaped area has a different color, such as the following:

YELLOW   RED   BLUE   GREEN   BLACK   BLANK

When the wheel is rotated, each color will appear between the mask at the upper center of the responder.

On the reverse side, the side which faces the student, the six pie shaped areas have a letter, number, or word designating a different response such as:

A	B	C	D	E	BLANK
1	2	3	4	5	
Yes	No				
Correct	Incorrect				

Thus, the letter, number, or word answer on one side matches and is identified by a color on the reverse side in this order:

YELLOW	means the answer			A, 1, Yes, or Correct
RED	”	”	”	B, 2, No, or Incorrect
BLUE	”	”	”	C, 3
GREEN	”	”	”	D, 4
BLACK	”	”	”	E, 5
BLANK	”			No response

With each student having one of these response devices, we see how the teacher can quickly, easily, and reliably go over the diagnostic test of each student and obtain a group assessment of performance on each test item or items for each objective. The teacher need simply say, *What is your answer to the first question?* Each student dials the answer as he or she has indicated on his or her copy of the test. The teacher looks out and sees colors (which indicate specific answers). If, for example, the correct answer to the first question is "A," then the color YELLOW should be seen, which would indicate mastery of a test item for an objective. If a rainbow effect is seen, this would indicate something else. Confidentiality is retained in that each student's answer is masked from other students, while at the same time a convenient and quick assessment by the teacher is obtained of group performance. In the *Design Format,* we will describe features related to the level of group performance that might be expected and considerations regarding the amount of time involved in actually carrying out this means of assessment. Be assured that the time needed for this assessment process is well within a limit that allows for classroom instruction to follow in the same class period.

Assembling the Lesson Plan

The fifth step in the CLP approach, Assembling the Lesson Plan, is a function that is carried out at the same time the diagnostic test is being scored through use of the response device. You will have to see the specific *Design Format* to grasp the ease with which this step is accomplished. Essentially, this will involve selecting out of the preplanned lesson those specific lesson items which relate to the objectives indicated by the diagnostic test as needing in-class instruction. It also involves coordinating those items selected out with what will become known as the Content Outline for the purpose of maintaining continuity of classroom instruction.

Implementation and Feedback

Operationally, the sixth step is Implementation and Feedback. One might well think that it is about time the CLP approach got around to what we normally think of as classroom instruction. The emphasis which will be given to implementation will have to do with capitalizing on the valuable selection process that has led up to this point. We have selected out those objectives with which the students need help because they have not learned such objectives on their own through preparatory study. Additional time should be available now because of this selection process, and it should be used to full advantage for learning effectiveness. In the *Design Format* section, which follows, it will be described how it is suggested that implementation and feedback be given. The author wishes to assure the reader that the CLP approach will allow the individual teacher to use whatever style and methods (e.g., lecture, discovery, discussion, etc.) that he or she is accustomed to using and has found effective.

III.

DESIGN FORMAT

The primary aim of any instructional approach is, of course, learning effectiveness. It should promote student learning to the fullest extent possible. This is the primary aim of the Construct Lesson Plan approach.

The design format for the CLP is composed of three components, illustrated for a sample lesson in Figures 2, 3, and 4; see Appendix. In order, these are labeled the Diagnostic Pretest, Lesson Plan Cards, and Content Outline. The complete sample lesson is one drawn from an introductory course in economics.

Pretest

The first three steps of the CLP approach are:
1. Preplanning
2. Preparatory Study
3. Diagnostic Testing

Preplanning by the teacher and preparatory study will henceforth be assumed as "givens." Assume that you, the teacher, have prepared a lesson based on the format design which is about to be described. Also assume that you have determined the means, say a chapter from a textbook, the students will use to prepare themselves for the lesson. You must now design the means for assessing what the students will have learned on their own. This will take the form of a diagnostic test, or pretest to classroom instruction.

In the sample lesson given in this text there are 13 objectives to a lesson on the topic of the *Theory of National Income Determination.* You may wish to familiarize yourself with these objectives in Figures 3.1 to 3.13 (see Appendix). This particular lesson is but one of several in an economics course that lasts one semester, and meets two hours for each lesson. The diagnostic pretest for this lesson, as shown in Figures 2.1 through 2.9 (see Appendix), is composed of test items sufficient to measure all 13 objectives. Each item has been determined to be an accurate test of whether or not the students would have mastered the objectives measured.

The first thing to note about this test is that the test items are all multiple-choice. Why is this so? Outside of the fact that multiple-choice items are generally good indicators of student performance on objectives (other than psychomotor, manipulative objectives), there is the practical matter of implementation. Multiple-choice questions can be quickly and easily *scored.* If the diagnostic pretest were composed of, say, essay questions, it would take a great deal of time to score the test. Little time would then be left over for classroom instruction.

The fact that the diagnostic pretest must be in the form of multiple-choice questioning does not preclude the use of some completion type and *brief* essay questions. The diagnostic test can include some of these, but it is recommended that they be few.

A second, although less compelling, reason for using multiple-choice test items relates to the confidentiality of student responding that was noted in the *Operational Description.* You will recall that a response device (Figure 1) is to be used in going over the test. When multiple-choice questions are posed, each student will dial on the response device his or her answer. With completion and essay questions, a representative answer would have to be given by the teacher; and the students would indicate on their response devices whether they answered correctly or not (by the use of the Yes or No answer segments of the response device). While confidentiality of individual student's response is not lost in this procedure for essay questions, the confidentiality of the *answer* is lost. If students in general did not exhibit the correct answer, then the correct answer would be given away— showing them the correct answer without any instruction. Thus, it is best to use multiple-choice questions for the pretest when possible. The CLP approach is limited in regard to assessing manipulative skills (as in electronics, science experiments, etc.), but these are objectives usually pursued instructionally on an individual basis rather than by group instruction. Background information and procedural steps to manipulative objectives can be approached by the Construct Lesson Plan design.

What we need for the diagnostic pretest is a set of test items, mostly multiple-choice in form, which test all of the objectives of a preplanned lesson. This means that there must be at least one test item for each objective. For some objectives, it will mean more than one test item to fully measure the objectives. You will note, for instance, in Figure 2.2 (see Appendix) that two test items are provided to measure objective number three. In Figure 2.1, objectives one and two are each measured by only one test item. The general guide is to provide, of course, the number of test items that are necessary to test the particular objective. In the sample lesson of 13 objectives, there are a total of 15 items. Even if there were twice this number of test items, there would still be time to go over the entire test and have plenty of time for instruction itself.

Let us suppose then that we have prepared our diagnostic pretest and that the students each have been given a copy. They are instructed to do their preparatory study. The night before the lesson is to be given in class, the students take a half hour or so to complete the test. Since this test is not going to be graded for achievement purposes, but rather to help the students ascertain what they have and have not learned and to *construct* a lesson plan, there is little, if any, likelihood that the students will *cheat,* for there is *no reason* to do so. The students perceive quite readily that they are only cheating themselves if they do.

At the beginning of the class period, the teacher then goes over the diagnostic test. The teacher simply asks the students for their answers to the first test item. Each student so indicates on his or her response device. The teacher looks out and assesses group performance on the first test item. For that test item (objective) the teacher has predetermined an acceptable group performance criteria that must be met to conclude that the students, as a group, have achieved the objective. This criteria might be, for example, 80 percent of the students (that is, 24 out of 30 students in our sample class of 30 students). For other test items and objectives, the criteria might be higher (90 percent) or lower (say, 70 percent) of the student group. One must remember that this is group instruction and not individual instruction, so a criterion of 100 percent is not reasonable. There might be an occasional objective requiring 100 percent of the students to demonstrate mastery, but it is likely that there will be few of these.

As the teacher proceeds through each test item and makes the assessment of group performance, it is important to observe the following two-step procedure:

    1. Any time the student group meets the criteria, the teacher should tell them that they have met the criteria and give the students the correct answer. This

reinforces a correct response and indicates to the students that they have learned the objective on their own. This objective will not require any or much classroom instruction.

2. Any time the student group *does not* meet the group criteria, then the teacher does not give the correct answer. Rather, the teacher simply informs the class that that objective will be covered in classroom instruction which is to follow.

In following the above procedure, the teacher can go quickly through the entire diagnostic test and assess which objectives the students have not learned. There will typically be little, if any, discussion between teacher and students at this point, as the idea is to quickly make the assessment upon which the instruction will be centered following the test. In repeated uses, the author has found that this assessment process typically takes under ten minutes and usually averages about six to eight minutes. In the early attempts at implementation of the procedure, it may take longer in that both teacher and students must become accustomed to what is mostly likely an entirely new approach to instruction. Students will often want to know the answer to all test items. Once they perceive, however, that the instruction which follows does deal with what they didn't learn on their own, they quickly see why such answers are not initially given to them.

The result of following a diagnostic testing model is that the teacher now knows (and the students also know) which objectives they have or have not learned. Classroom instruction will center on the latter set of objectives. A savings in classroom instructional time is evident by this procedure. How does the teacher now put together a lesson plan, from a total preplanned plan, which will center on those objectives requiring attention? This is where the previously labeled *lesson plan cards* come into use.

Lesson Plan Cards

Lesson Plan Cards are intended to allow the teacher a convenient means for complete preplanning of a lesson and yet the flexibility to select out of this full preplanning those parts of the lesson which will actually be used in class as a result of the diagnostic pretesting. The lesson plan cards for the sample lesson being used as an illustration are to be found in Figures 3.1 through 3.13 (see Appendix).

You will first note that there are 13 lesson plan cards— one for each objective of this lesson. There is a number for each card in the upper right hand corner. Each card contains the following features:

- Card Number
- Content Heading (Topic and Subtopics)
- Objective
- Answer(s)
- Notes
- Enabling Questions

The card number identifies the objective. This is purely for organizational purposes. It allows the teacher to keep the cards in order, for they will be rearranged according to the needs of the individual class and will need to be reassembled for the next class (assuming there is more than one). Also, this arrangement allows the teacher to sequence the cards in another order if so desired. If more than one teacher were using the sample set of cards, each teacher could sequence the cards as he or she might desire. The card numbers match the numbers assigned to the test items in the diagnostic pretest.

The Content Headings, labeled Topic and Subtopic, are also for organizational and orientation purposes. Since the cards are organized around individual learner objectives, one or more objectives will be found within a given content heading. For instances, under the topic heading of *Invest-*

ment and Income in Figures 3.1, 3.2, and 3.3, there are three objectives.

Traditional lesson plans are organized around content headings. The problem with content headings is that they don't clearly communicate what is expected of students; and, indeed, to several teachers a content heading might lead to many different interpretations of what is to be taught. On the other hand, objectives narrow the content outcomes, and add how the students will demonstrate mastery of the content. In other words, objectives are a communications device between teacher and students.

The Notes section of a lesson plan card is where the teacher will specify any special content reminders, activities, visuals, exercises, and so forth, that he or she would need to be reminded of for *potential* use with students. It is *potential* in that use will depend on what the teacher thinks he or she needs at the time of instruction.

The Enabling Questions section of the lesson plan cards is reserved for a special type of questioning which the teacher may wish to utilize in addition to the questions used in the diagnostic test. This type of questioning will be used *during* instruction, rather than before (as with the diagnostic test) or after (as with review or achievement testing) instruction in the classroom.

Enabling questions are simply those the teacher might want to ask to clarify certain items along the path of learning an objective. Such questioning would give the teacher an idea of whether the students are comprehending information prior to going to the next step or before a question which would require the students to demonstrate mastery of the objective itself. For example, to the objective in Figure 3.1, the teacher might well stop at a certain point and ask the students to "Define National Income." This question would be written on the lesson plan in the Enabling Question section. However, although it is written there, it is not required that it be used. The teacher may well sense that, through discussion, the students have a grasp of the definition and need not be asked the enabling question. In general terms, what is needed as enabling questions can be discovered by the questions that students ask. Thus, in using a lesson plan it is a good idea to take the time and record after instruction some of the questions students always seem to ask and incorporate these into the lesson plan as Enabling Questions.

Finally, although its use is obvious enough, there is on the lesson plan a space provided for the Answers to the diagnostic test. You see this in the example in Figure 3.1 immediately following the objective. This is provided so that the lesson plan card can be used as the source for answers to the diagnostic test. Thus, as the diagnostic test is being scored at the beginning of class, the function of dividing the lesson plan cards into two stacks of *know* and *don't know* objectives can be accomplished. The lesson plan can be *constructed* at the same time as test *assessment* is occurring.

Content Outline

Following what has been described thus far, the teacher could then proceed with instruction. The method of instruction could be in any form or combination of forms he or she might choose—lecture, discussion, case, discovery, etc. However, the selection procedure of narrowing in on specific objectives needing classroom attention usually results in the selection of objectives from here and there within the total lesson rather than a sequential set of objectives. For example, from the sample lesson that has been used let us suppose that the diagnostic test has resulted in the following set of objectives needing classroom instruction: 2, 4, 5, 8, 10, and 13.

If we were to proceed with classroom instruction on only these six particular objectives, then there is a chance that instruction would be fragmented and lacking continuity. Covering only these objectives would be out of context with the other seven objectives. Correctly assuming that any given lesson is usually an integrated unit of content around a central major topic, as in this case, *The Theory of National Income Determination,* it would not be prudent to fragment the total lesson by centering instruction on only the six objectives needing specific attention. In order to avoid such fragmentation, the Content Outline is used in conjunction with the lesson plan cards.

Figure 4 (see Appendix) illustrates a typical Content Outline used in the CLP approach. The outline is much the same as one would normally see in a textbook. The one addition to this outline is an indication in the left margin of where the specific objectives of the lesson relate to the content. Thus, the 13 objectives of the economics lesson have been keyed as to where they fall within the outline. Assuming that the six objectives listed above were the ones isolated by diagnostic testing as needing classroom instruction, you will note in Figure 4 that these six objectives have been circled in the outline. We are now ready to see how implementation would proceed with the use of the lesson plan cards and content outline.

Visualize that the teacher has before him or her a Content Outline as a guide. The teacher opens the lesson with a general introduction to the lesson—possibly reviewing the overall goals to be achieved. The teacher then notes the first content item on the outline and sees that the first objective has already been achieved by the students. The teacher would briefly cover this first objective in an overview manner, since the students have already learned the objectives on their own. When the teacher gets to the second objective, one which the students have not mastered (and he would know this because it is circled on the Content Outline) he proceeds

from the Outline to the lesson plan card on this objective
(#2). This card would be the first one on top of the stack of
lesson plan cards. Instead of an overview approach to this objective, specific instruction would be given, guided by the lesson plan card. Content reminders, media suggestions, activities, exercises, and enabling questions are readily available for
reminding the teacher as to what might be done in the way of
instruction. After such instruction, the teacher may wish to
ask the diagnostic test item again so as to assess if the student
group has now learned the objective. If the students have
done so, the teacher then goes on to the next objective (in
this case, objective #3). The teacher in turn notes that the
students have learned objective #3 and provides an overview/
review. Then, the teacher moves on to objective #4, the next
lesson plan card, and on through all the objectives of the
lesson. What you observe happening is an *informational*,
general overview coverage of objectives already learned by
students and a specific *instructional* approach to objectives
on which students need classroom attention. Continuity is
achieved by use of the Content Outline and specific instruction by the Lesson Plan Cards. The combined effect is
instructional efficiency and effectiveness.

Implementation in General

   A general recommendation has been made regarding the
way in which instruction might proceed using the CLP approach. In brief terms, it was suggested that a generic, overview approach, labeled an *Informational* approach, be taken
to objectives already learned by students through their
preparatory study. A more detailed, *Instructional* approach is
taken to objectives which require classroom coverage, guided
by the lesson plan cards. While the distinction of general
versus specific is useful for pointing out the functional
difference between Content Outline and Lesson Plan Cards,

further clarification of what is involved in an *Instructional Approach* would be useful. As a base of comparison, an *Informational Approach,* using the Content Outline, means an overview, summary approach to content. Students may wish to ask their own questions to clarify what they feel needs further clarification, but the teacher is less apt to require and ask questions (i.e., for testing mastery of the objectives).

An instructional approach to objectives the students have yet to master requires all of the following:

1. Content coverage, through lecture, discussion, discovery, or other such means, in enough depth to discern that the students have come to learn the objective under study. This may or may not be supported by audio and visual means, exercises, and practice requirements on an individual or group basis. Such content and activities as are needed would be briefly outlined in the Notes section of the Lesson Plan Cards for ready access.

2. During #1 above, the students would be encouraged to ask clarifying questions. In like manner, the teacher might employ the use of his or her own enabling questions to check student progress towards achievement of an objective under study.

3. At a convenient point, in the judgment of the teacher, the students would be required to demonstrate they have learned the objective as a result of engaging in #1 and #2 above. This could be done through use of the original diagnostic test item(s) or suitable alternative test items the teacher makes available (and which would be specified on the lesson plan cards). The teacher would then indicate the correctness or incorrectness of group performance.

As a final note on implementation, while an objective by objective approach has been suggested, it has not been the intent to suggest that the teacher must proceed with one objective, then the next, and so on. Rather, it is more likely that the teacher would wish to cover several objectives before ascertaining student mastery. Indeed, a teacher may prefer to go through an entire lesson and leave to the very end of the class the determination of mastery. This is less likely, however, since many lessons are cumulative in nature, and to understand the latter part of a lesson requires understanding of the first and middle parts. As an example, you will note in Figure 4 (see Appendix) that the lesson is divided into three major areas. It is more likely that the teacher would prefer to teach the objectives within these three areas, rather than one objective after the other. The first area, *Investment and Income,* contains two objectives that have already been mastered (#1 and #3) and one objective that has not been mastered (#2). Structured interaction for objective #2 might immediately follow instruction on this objective or after informational coverage on objective #3 (or even later in the lesson).

In summarizing the CLP approach, the following checklist on implementation of the CLP approach will be useful in reviewing the instructional components.

CLP Implementation Checklist

Diagnostic Test
...... Establish group criteria for each question by weighing the relative importance of the objective it tests.

...... Give answers only when group criteria is met.

...... Regive the questions and provide answer during instruction or use a suitable substitute question.

...... Answers are on Lesson Plan Cards.

...... Lesson Plan Card numbers match test item numbers.

...... Use the Pretest as an indicator to find out who is doing effective preparatory study.

...... If a student has not answered a question(s) in advance, he or she can place the response wheel down on the table.

...... Students complete the test prior to coming to class, and after doing their preparatory study.

...... Ask students not to compare their answers prior to going over the test in class.

...... Ask students not to change answers after referring to preparatory study materials.

...... The teacher should use no more than 10 minutes to go over the test with students at the beginning of class. This time also includes assembling the Lesson Plan Cards and marking the Content Outline.

...... Use test results as indicators of areas needing revision with preparatory materials and lesson plan visuals, enabling questions, practice needs, etc.

...... The PURPOSE of the Diagnostic Test is to find out which objectives the students, as a group, have and have not mastered on their own.

Lesson Plan Cards
...... Personalize the cards by writing your own notes, questions, visual specifications, etc., in advance.

...... Use for instructional purposes.

...... Write and use enabling questions.

...... Divide cards as you go over the Diagnostic Test. Answers are on cards.

...... Coordinate card numbers with Content Outline.

...... State the objective to the class prior to beginning instruction on the objective.

...... The PURPOSE of the Lesson Plan Cards is to narrow instruction to objectives of immediate difficulty to the students, thus improving classroom instructional efficiency and providing more time for learning effectiveness.

Content Outline:
...... Use for informational purposes.

...... Allow other teachers to personalize the Content Outline if preferred. Make sure all objectives are keyed within the Content Outline.

...... Circle on the Content Outline the Lesson Plan Cards to be used (as a result of the Pretest).

...... Coordinate with Lesson Plan Cards by circling objective number needing classroom instruction.

...... The PURPOSE of the Content Outline is to assure a continuity (cohesiveness) of instruction.

General
...... Watch for evolving pattern indicating students who may not be studying or who seem to need additional help, as indicated by Diagnostic answers.

...... Allow the students, of course, to freely ask their own questions.

...... Keep in mind that the intent is to concentrate the class time available on objectives the students have not mastered (as indicated by the Diagnostic results).

...... Objective number, Lesson Plan Card number, and Pretest number should all correspond to each other.

...... Provide the students with a list of learner objectives for completing their preparatory study. Key reference sources to objectives.

IV.

OUTCOMES

The emphasis throughout this book has been on how the CLP approach improves teaching efficiency. It is, however, learning effectiveness and teaching effectiveness which are the ultimate outcomes we would hope to achieve in classroom instruction. In general, the CLP approach improves upon efficiency, thus allowing the teacher more time to devote to effectiveness; at the same time, the instructional design itself has many features which promote effectiveness of learning and teaching:

1. The Construct Lesson Plan approach promotes learning and teaching effectiveness because it provides a convenient and ready assessment of the immediate learning needs of students (relative to the learner objectives). This is due to giving the teacher a means (the diagnostic pretest) to assess objectives on which students need help. Effectiveness of teaching (and learning) is improved by the opportunity to devote classroom time and effort to these objectives and by avoiding (although not ignoring) those objectives the students have already learned.

2. The diagnostic Pretest and objectives promote student self-questioning during classroom instruction. Since each student knows what he or she has and has not achieved (as evidenced by Pretest results) the student has a basis upon

which to explore (through in-class questioning) that which has not been learned.

3. The Construct Lesson Plan promotes effectiveness because it structures questioning within the classroom. That is, in implementing the Construct Lesson Plan, the teacher is advised to reuse the Pretest item(s) once instructional activities (e.g., discussion, lecturing, practice, use of media, etc.) have been employed. This provides the means necessary for the teacher to *check* on instructional effectiveness. If learning effectiveness has not been achieved (as evidenced by use of alternative test items or reuse of the Pretest items), then the teacher can provide additional instruction or refer the students to remedial sources. The premise is that the teacher should *test* for effectiveness *in* the classroom and make adjustments, rather than waiting to make judgments later, such as after achievement testing (which is too late). Structured questioning is a *must* to improving teaching effectiveness.

4. The CLP approach calls for providing feedback to students as to the correctness or incorrectness of their learning. This is done both for the Pretest and reuse of test items in the classroom. As a result, there is a reinforcement provided when correct answers are given. Reinforcement is an essential feature of effectiveness and the CLP approach assures that reinforcement is given.

5. The CLP approach utilizes *enabling* (helping) questions to monitor student progress towards achievement of objectives. This process promotes teaching effectiveness in that it gives the teacher feedback as to the specific progress being made by students towards learning various aspects (steps, procedures, background information, etc.) of a particular objective under discussion. While enabling questions are not used continuously, they are particularly useful in checking progress towards difficult objectives, and serve

the teacher in determining precisely where the students are having difficulty learning.

6. Teaching effectiveness can be enhanced, to a certain degree, by resequencing instruction. In using the Construct Lesson Plan, teachers can easily resequence instruction by shifting the Lesson Plan Cards and by the development of their own Content Outline (as the second major component of the CLP). Thus, teaching effectiveness is improved to the extent that the individual teacher can personalize the lesson plan, thus lessening the feeling on the teacher's part that this is *somebody else's*.

7. Learning effectiveness is improved for the student because the CLP approach provides the means for the teacher to identify which students need remedial assistance. This is possible because of the continual assessment process (both pretesting and in-class testing). Instruction, as such, does not end at the close of the class period. Assuming that the students learned many objectives on their own, and little time is needed in class to provide instruction on a group basis, then there is a further opportunity to work with students individually or in small groups in the classroom.

8. The CLP approach can help to improve teaching effectiveness by reliably identifying learning needs which are more effectively met by other media forms (other than teacher and written preparatory materials). That is, as this approach is used, it is usually the case that certain objectives will continue to *fall out* as, for whatever reason, being difficult to learn *vis-a-vis* the written preparatory materials or within the explanation and activities of the spoken word in the classroom. These might be solved by other instructional means used in or outside of the classroom. In effect, this approach should begin to isolate which objectives need to be learned by audio-visual means. Thus, the CLP approach improves effectiveness by assisting in identifying which objectives

cannot be learned inside or outside of the classroom by the more conventional means of instruction.

9. The CLP approach also improves teaching effectiveness because it has a built-in validation process which can be used by the teacher to judge the relative effectiveness of instruction. Assuming the Pretest tells the teacher that the students have not learned a particular objective, and the teacher then follows with instruction and reuses the Pretest item, then the teacher has an assessment of the effect of his or her instruction. Obviously, if the students are still not able to evidence achievement of an objective, after the teacher has guided learning in the classroom, then some adjustments are in order. These adjustments are part of the validation process. The CLP approach has this validation built in.

10. Effectiveness is also improved by getting students involved (which also means committed) in instruction by a variety of means. Although alluded to earlier, the emphasis here is in terms of how the CLP approach gets the students involved initially in the selection of objectives towards which the instruction will be directed in the classroom. It is the students, through their own performance as a group, who determine the focus of classroom instruction. Indeed, the CLP approach may be the first time a student has been given the opportunity to participate in the selection process, other than in a more general way. To the extent that students can become involved in instruction (on a structured or unstructured basis), the effectiveness of instruction should be improved.

11. One of the assumptions that is felt to lead to improving teaching effectiveness is having students in the classroom who have adequately prepared by completing assigned preparatory study materials. One of the reasons students do not come adequately prepared is that they do not generally perceive the immediate need to do so. Rather, they wait until

just before achievement test time and *cram* study. If one of the strongest motivations for getting students to come prepared is testing, then the CLP approach should assure that this has taken place. Indeed, experience has shown that it does. Effectiveness is thus promoted by students who come to class more adequately prepared. It is not only the fact that a test is being used, but also the recognition on the student's part that his or her preparatory study will be accounted for by the teacher. In effect, the teacher is saying, *You (the student) do the preparatory study and I (the teacher) will account for it.* Such accounting, for the student, is a positive contingency payoff for doing his or her preparatory study.

12. To the same degree that the CLP approach improves teaching effectiveness by allowing the teacher to personalize the lesson plan to his or her own needs, it also allows the individual teacher to utilize his or her own teaching style. The CLP approach is an overall organizational, administrative, and implementation procedure, but it does not preclude in any way the use of individual teaching styles such as lecturing, discovery, discussion, and so forth. In effect, it doesn't interfere with existing teaching effectiveness, but rather adds to it.

13. Finally, the CLP approach allows the teacher to identify problems in an aspect of learning which, while not part of the classroom, are part of the total learning effort of students. That is, the CLP approach, through use of the Pretest, is an indication of the effectiveness of preparatory study materials. While the Diagnostic Test is a Pretest to classroom instruction, it is a Posttest to preparatory study and should indicate where preparatory study materials need revision for effectiveness. To the extent that preparatory study can be improved, it should have a resulting effect of allowing additional time for in-class effectiveness.

V.

DEVELOPMENTAL GUIDE

The development of a Construct Lesson Plan is a relatively easy matter, although it can be time-consuming. Most of the time will be in developing and checking the reliability of the diagnostic test. In this regard, in some subject areas, such as mathematics, reading and communications skills, science, social studies, business education, and others, the developer might do well to check into some of the existing sources which provide *banks* of objectives and test items from which one can select many objectives and test items, and then develop his or her own for what is not available. Some of the sources include:

ORBIT: Objective-Referenced Bank of Items and Tests
California Test Bureau
McGraw-Hill, Inc.
Monterey, California 93940

IOX: Instructional Objectives Exchange
Post Office Box 24095
Los Angeles, California 90024

SCORE: School Curriculum Objective-Referenced Evaluation
Educational Services
Westinghouse Learning Corporation
P.O. Box 30
Iowa City, Iowa 52240

Most services are available at a nominal cost, and information may be obtained by writing directly to the sources indicated.

The developmental guide, which appears in Table 1 (next page), may be summarized as follows:

1. Learner objectives, while not an absolute requirement, do make the organization and implementation of the CLP approach much easier. They should be written to set the learning needs of students and to guide the implementation needs of the teacher. Their primary aim is for effective communication to students of what is expected of them from a course of study.

2. The diagnostic test is written after the objectives in order to quantify and clarify the objectives. The questions will help to provide many insights into what should be in the lesson in terms of content reminders, activities, projects, exercises, and needed media support.

3. Although the test items are written to the objectives on a one to one basis, it is worth noting that once a diagnostic test is written, a check can be made of any overlap or missed testing needs. Since the diagnostic test is a *selecting out* process, one must be careful that the test is complete in measuring the full intent and outcomes expected from the lesson.

4. Sequence can be an important aspect of learning. In this step the teacher is to determine what will probably be the best sequence, subject to possible alteration during the following implementation. Since the lesson plan cards can be resequenced with relative ease, it can be anticipated that actual implementation may indicate that the initial sequence is not *the best.* Sequencing at this point in development is largely for organizational needs in that the learner objectives and test items must be coordinated for use with students and in the subsequent *constructing* of the lesson plan.

Table 1

Developmental Guide to
Construct Lesson Plan

	Lesson #	1	2	3	4	5
1. Write Learner Objectives						
2. Write Diagnostic Test Items						
3. Objectives and Test Item Approval						
4. Sequence Objectives and Assign Numbers						
5. Develop Content Outline and Key Objectives						
6. Develop Lesson Plan Cards						
Card Number						
Percentage Criteria for Test Items						
Topic and Subtopic						
Objective						
Pretest Answers (letter and color)						
Fill in Notes (if for self)						
Write Enabling Questions						
7. Implement						
8. Check reliability of test items						

5. Although from the very outset the teacher may have a good idea of an outline of the subject matter, the Content Outline and keying of objectives (by number) within it should be completed at this stage of development. Some of the information from the Content Outline, specifically the topic headings, will be used to complete the next step of preparing the individual lesson plan cards. Of course, this initial outline can be modified with relative ease based on actual tryout.

6. Development of the lesson plan cards is an easy matter in that most parts of the cards have already been developed in prior steps. It is suggested that a master card be printed and copies made which can then be filled in with numbers, objective statements, pretest answers, and other needs. If you are developing the lesson plan for your own use, the Notes section can be filled in as you require. If you are developing lesson plan cards for other teachers to use, the Notes section should be left blank so that each individual teacher might specify his or her own needs. In this way, the lesson plan can be personalized by each teacher and will more likely, as such, be actually used. The developer also may wish to specify certain enabling questions if he or she is developing the lesson for other teachers to use. However, this should be kept to a minimum. The individual teacher should be encouraged to specify what he or she thinks is needed. Much of this may have to await actual implementation, in which questions asked by students in class are a good source of what is needed in the way of enabling questions.

7. After the first time, implementation of a CLP will show some needed changes and additions. Some adjustments in the number of objectives in a lesson, for instance, may show up. This could mean adding more objectives in that the preparatory study is doing a satisfactory job of promoting learning. It could mean the opposite—taking out some objectives and

placing them in subsequent assignments. More likely, however, is the addition of specific needs in certain lesson plan cards where it is found that students are having difficulty with certain objectives.

8. Finally, a special note is made in the Developmental Guide to check on the reliability of diagnostic test items. Much of how this is done will have to be obtained from texts that are available on testing procedures. In general, whether the diagnostic test is reliable will be indicated by subsequent achievement tests that the teacher will give for grading purposes. It is worth emphasizing here that while the *grades* of achievement tests are important, the teacher should be especially watchful for indications in the achievement tests which show whether the students knew (for example, from preparatory study) objectives in the first place.

In summarizing development, it should be said that development of a CLP approach need not be done all at once. It can be a gradual process of development and introduction. Objectives can be written and used one year. Then a diagnostic test developed and used and reliability checked. Development and use of Lesson Plan Cards and the Content Outline can follow. Lessons can be planned initially on a weekly basis, then subdivided for two-day or one-day sessions.

VI.

RESOURCES

The Construct Lesson Plan is a relatively new instructional design. It was researched, developed, and evaluated at The American College, Bryn Mawr, Pennsylvania. Additional descriptive information is available from the following sources:

BOOKS

Langdon, Danny G. *Interactive Instructional Designs for Individualized Learning.* Englewood Cliffs, N.J.: Educational Technology Publications, Inc., 1973.

Evans, Lionel and Leedham, John. *Aspects of Educational Technology IX.* London, England: Kogan Page Limited, 1975.

ARTICLES

Langdon, Danny G., The Construct Lesson Plan: Improving Instructional Efficiency. *Educational Technology,* April, 1975, 19-23.

Langdon, Danny G., The Construct Lesson Plan: Taking the Inefficiency Out of Group/Classroom Instruction. *PLET Journal,* Vol. 14, No. 3, August, 1977, 199-206.

IN USE AT

As of the date of this publication, the CLP approach is being used in approximately 100 classrooms in an Economics course which is taught at locations throughout the United States. Descriptive information about this course may be obtained from The American College, Bryn Mawr, Pennsylvania 19010.

WORKSHOP

The author conducts a one-day workshop on the CLP approach.

VIDEOTAPE

An introductory videotape of the CLP is available, at handling costs only, from The American College, Bryn Mawr, Pennsylvania 19010. This 15-minute videocassette introduces the need for and basic components of the approach, with a demonstration in a classroom. Details may be obtained by writing to The American College.

VII.

APPENDIX

Figure 1

Wheel Responder

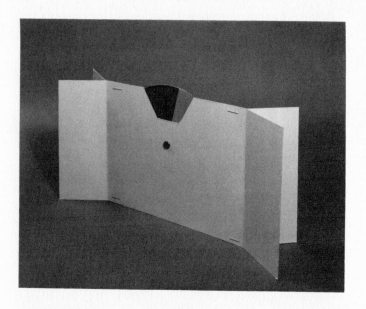

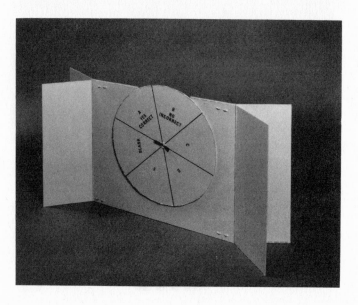

Figure 1
(Continued)

Materials Needed
8-ply board
Very thin paper in five colors
Brass Paper Fasteners (½")
Stapler, Marking Pen, Compass, Ruler, Scissors

Directions
1. Cut the 8-ply board into 16" x 11" pieces for as many wheel responders as you wish to make.
2. Using a compass and ruler, mark off the dimensions shown below.

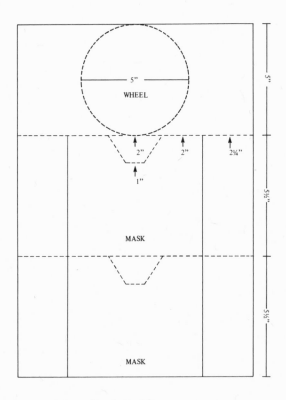

3. Cut out areas along the dotted lines.

Figure 1
(Continued)

4. Using one of the wheels you have cut out, or the compass, draw a circle on each piece of colored paper the size of the wheel. The circle you have drawn is to be divided into six pie shaped pieces. One pie shaped color will go on one response wheel, so cut only one circle to make six response wheels. For example, if you want to make 30 responders, draw only five circles; divide each into six equal pie shapes, and you will then have 30 individual pie shaped pieces, one for each response wheel. Do this for each of the five different colors.

5. Place one of each pie shaped color on the wheel in the order shown below. Note that one pie shaped area is left on the wheel for a blank position.

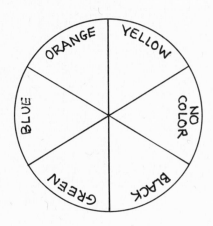

6. Using a ball point pen or similar sharp object, punch a small hole in the very center of the wheel, large enough for a brass fastener to go through.

7. On the reverse side of the wheel, use a marking pen to divide the wheel into six pie shaped areas exactly corresponding to the colored areas on the other side. Each area should be labeled as follows:

Figure 1
(Continued)

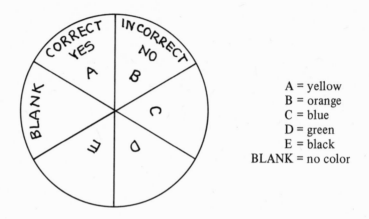

A = yellow
B = orange
C = blue
D = green
E = black
BLANK = no color

8. To construct the stand, simply place the two masks one over the other, and staple in the four position as shown here:

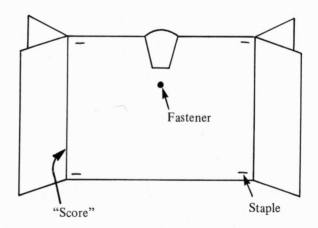

Figure 1
(Continued)

9. Lay the mask flat on a table and score slightly along the solid lines. Bend the flaps apart and the mask will stand firmly.

10. Position the wheel on the mask, such that when the wheel is rotated, each color will appear evenly between the cut out area of the mask. Punch a hole through the mask where the hole in the center of the wheel is located. Use a brass fastener to secure the wheel to the mask.

Figure 2.1

HS 304   ASSIGNMENT 5
ECONOMICS

PRETEST

1. Which of the following statements correctly describe(s) the effect of
   an upward shift in scheduled saving if scheduled investment remains
   constant?
     I.   Consumption decreases and GNP decreases.
     II.   Consumption remains constant and GNP remains constant.
     III. GNP falls by more than the increase in scheduled saving.
     IV. GNP rises by the amount of increased scheduled saving.
     V.   GNP falls to the level at which people desire to save what
         the system can invest.
       ...... A. I and III only
       ...... B. II only
       ...... C. IV only
       ...... D. I, III, and V only
       ...... E. V only

2. All the following statements concerning induced investment and
   autonomous investment are correct EXCEPT:
     ...... A. Induced investment results from accelerated deprecia-
           tion methods which reduce taxes and induce business
           firms to invest more in plant and equipment.
     ...... B. Autonomous investment results from changes in vari-
           bles other than employment, production, and national
           income.
     ...... C. Induced investment is depicted on the saving-and-invest-
           ment diagram as an upward-sloping schedule that in-
           creases as GNP increases.
     ...... D. Autonomous investment is depicted on the saving-and-
           investment diagram as a horizontal line that remains
           constant throughout the entire range of GNP.
     ...... E. Induced investment is related to changes in income, and
           autonomous investment is independent of changes in
           income.

Figure 2.2

ASSIGNMENT 5   HS 304
                                                    ECONOMICS

3a. The "paradox of thrift" states that
...... A.   an increase in scheduled saving could result in higher
            consumption, thereby increasing GNP
...... B.   an increase in scheduled saving could result in lower con-
            sumption, investment, and GNP, thereby causing total
            saving to decline
...... C.   a decrease in scheduled saving could cause consumption,
            investment, and GNP to increase, thereby causing total
            saving to exceed investment
...... D.   if scheduled saving increases, investment remains con-
            stant, causing GNP to remain constant
...... E.   an increase in scheduled saving could result in higher
            consumption, investment, and GNP, thereby causing
            total saving to increase

3b.   Which of the following statements correctly explain the effect of
      thriftiness on national income?
   I.   If the economy is at a depressed level, thrift is a social vir-
        tue which induces business firms to increase investment.
  II.   If the economy is at an inflated level, an increase in planned
        thrift causes income to become available for investment
        through a decline in consumption, thereby causing a greater
        rate of inflation.
 III.   If the economy is at a depressed level, an increase in
        planned thrift causes investment and national income to
        fall.
  IV.   If the economy is at an inflated level, an increase in planned
        thrift causes consumption to fall, thereby reducing infla-
        tionary pressures.
   V.   An increase in planned thrift causes GNP to fall if the
        economy is at a depressed level and causes GNP to remain
        constant if the economy is at an inflated level.
        ...... A.   I and II only
        ...... B.   II and III only
        ...... C.   III and IV only
        ...... D.   IV and V only
        ...... E.   I, II, and V only

Figure 2.3

HS 304   ASSIGNMENT 5
ECONOMICS

4. A "deflationary gap" is
...... A.   an excess of C + I spending over GNP at full employ-
            ment and causes the economy to seek equilibrium at a
            higher GNP level
...... B.   an excess of C + I spending over GNP at full employ-
            ment and causes the economy to seek equilibrium at a
            lower GNP level
...... C.   an excess of GNP over C + I spending at full employ-
            ment and causes the conomy to seek equilibrium at a
            higher GNP level
...... D.   an excess of GNP over C + I spending at full employ-
            ment and causes the economy to seek equilibrium at a
            lower GNP level
...... E.   an excess of C + I over C + S at full employment and
            causes the economy to seek equilibrium at a lower GNP
            level

5. An "inflationary gap" is
...... A.   an excess of C + I spending over GNP at full employ-
            ment and causes prices to fall
...... B.   an excess of S over I at full employment and causes
            prices to rise
...... C.   an excess of GNP over C + I spending at full employ-
            ment and causes prices to rise
...... D.   an excess of I over S at full employment and causes
            prices to rise
...... E.   an excess of C + S over C + I at full employment and
            causes prices to rise

Figure 2.4

ASSIGNMENT 5   HS 304
        ECONOMICS

6. All the following statements correctly explain how deflationary and inflationary gaps are measured EXCEPT:

     ...... A.   Using the consumption-plus-investment diagram, a deflationary gap is measured by the excess of GNP over C + I at full employment.

     ...... B.   Using the saving-and-investment diagram, a deflationary gap is measured by the excess of S over I at full employment.

     ...... C.   Using the consumption-plus-investment diagram, an inflationary gap is measured by the excess of total spending over GNP at the inflationary equilibrium level.

     ...... D.   Using the saving-and-investment diagram, an inflationary gap is measured by the excess of I over S at full employment.

     ...... E.   The gaps are never measured at any level of GNP except the full employment level.

Figure 2.5

Use the following diagrams to answer Question 7:

(1)   (2)

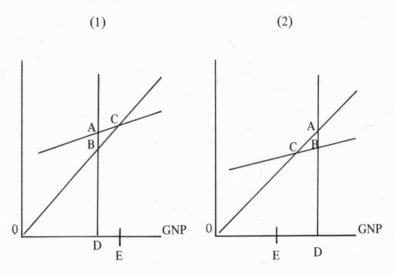

7. Assuming that lines OD represent the level of full employment GNP,
   which of the following statements concerning deflationary gaps and
   inflationary gaps are correct?
   I.   Diagram (1) illustrates an inflationary gap because DE mea-
         sures the excess of total spending over total income.
   II.   Diagram (2) illustrates a deflationary gap and AB measures
         the excess of full employment saving over investment.
   III. Diagram (1) illustrates a deflationary gap because AB mea-
         sures the excess of full employment saving over investment.
   IV.   Diagram (2) illustrates a deflationary gap and ED measures
         the excess of total spending over total income.
   V.   Diagram (1) illustrates an inflationary gap because AB mea-
         sures the excess of full employment investment over saving.
         ...... A.   I and II only
         ...... B.   I and IV only
         ...... C.   II and III only
         ...... D.   II and V only
         ...... E.   IV and V only

Figure 2.6

ASSIGNMENT 5   HS 304
                                                ECONOMICS

8. All the following statements concerning demand-pull inflation are
   correct EXCEPT:
   ...... A. Excess purchasing power results in price increases.
   ...... B. The quantity of goods produced at full employment and
              offered for sale is inadequate in relation to the money
              demand, thereby causing prices to increase.
   ...... C. Real GNP cannot move above the maximum full em-
              ployment level, but money GNP increases because prices
              rise when aggregate demand exceeds aggregate supply.
   ...... D. Equilibrium never is reached in the case of demand-pull
              inflation because higher prices generate higher incomes
              which generate higher demand and higher prices in a
              spiral-effect upwards.
   ...... E. Production costs are too high in relation to total spend-
              ing, thereby causing prices to rise when business firms
              try to prevent profit-erosion.

9. "Fiscal policy" consists of
   ..... A.   governmental measures affecting the money supply, the
              major purpose being to change interest rates
   ...... B. governmental measures involving taxes and expenditures,
              the major purpose being to change the equilibrium level
              of income
   ...... C. governmental tax and revenue measures aimed at bal-
              ancing the federal budget
   ...... D. governmental tax and spending measures aimed at bal-
              ancing the federal budget without causing inflation or
              deflation
   ...... E. government monetary measures aimed at controlling
              interest rates and causing a desirable redistribution of
              national income

Figure 2.7

HS 304   ASSIGNMENT 5
ECONOMICS

Use the following diagram to answer Question 10:

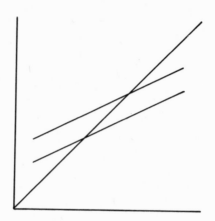

10. Which of the following statements correctly explain the effect of
    adding "G" to "C + I" when using the 45-degree line diagram
    shown above?
    I.   Total spending consists of C + I + G.
    II. The C + I + G curve (or line) is parallel to the C + I curve
         (or line).
    III. Adding "G" shifts the equilibrium level of GNP upward.
    IV. Equilibrium GNP is determined by the intersection of the
         C + I curve and the 45-degree line because "G" is just offset
         by taxes which act as leakage from the system.
    V.   Equilibrium GNP is determined by the intersection of the
         C + I + G curve and the 45-degree line because "G" repre-
         sents total government spending on goods and services,
         holding taxes constant.
         ...... A.   I and II only
         ...... B.   I, II, and III only
         ...... C.   I, II, III, and IV only
         ...... D.   I, II, III, and V only
         ...... E.   II, III, and IV only

Figure 2.8

11a. An increase in government expenditure, holding all other factors
constant, will cause
...... A. GNP to increase by the amount of increased government spending
...... B. GNP to increase by more than the increased government spending, the exact amount determined by the
value of the multiplier.
...... C. a chain of respending to be set in motion, causing
inflation
...... D. a chain of respending to be set in motion, causing
C + I to decline in an amount just equal to the increased government spending.
...... E. GNP and DI to increase while C, I, and S remain
constant

11b. All the following statements correctly explain the effect that a
change in taxes will have on both Gross National Product (GNP)
and disposable income (DI), when all other factors are held constant EXCEPT:
...... A. A tax increase reduces DI causing saving (S) to fall,
and GNP rise through secondary spending since investment (I) exceeds (S).
...... B. A tax increase reduces DI, thereby causing both consumption (C) and GNP to fall.
...... C. A tax increase helps to close the inflationary gap by
reducing consumption (C), shifting the consumption
schedule downward to the right, and causing GNP to
fall.
...... D. A tax decrease results in more DI, higher consumption (C), and higher GNP.
...... E. A tax decrease results in more DI, and higher money
GNP through inflation if the economy is at full employment, but real GNP does not rise.

Figure 2.9

HS 304   ASSIGNMENT 5
ECONOMICS

12. Assuming the MPC for the national economy is .8, and all other
    factors are held constant, to reduce an inflationary gap of $40
    billion, personal income taxes must be increased by
    ...... A. $ 5 billion
    ...... B. $ 8 billion
    ...... C. $10 billion
    ...... D. $40 billion
    ...... E. $50 billion

13. Which of the following statements correctly state the effect of a
    $10 billion increase in government expenditures (G) financed by a
    new $10 billion increase in personal income taxes (T), if the MPC
    for the national economy is .8, and all other factors are held
    constant?
    I.   The value of the multiplier is 4 and the increase in G results
          in a total increase of $40 billion in GNP.
    II.   The increase in T results in an initial increase in consump-
          tion spending (C) of $8 billion.
    III. The size of the drop in GNP resulting from the tax increase
          is less than the size of the rise in GNP resulting from the
          increased government spending.
    IV.   The net change in GNP resulting from both the increase in
          G and the increase in T is a rise of $10 billion.
    V.   The net change in GNP resulting from both the increase in
          G and the increase in T is a drop of $2 billion.
          ...... A.   I, II, and III only
          ...... B.   II, III, and IV only
          ...... C.   II, III, and V only
          ...... D.   I and II only
          ...... E.   III and IV only

Figure 3.1

HS 304 ECONOMICS	CARD # 1
	SUGGESTED % 80

Assignment   5   THEORY OF NATIONAL INCOME DE-
TERMINATION (CONCLUDED)

Topic   Investment and Income

Subtopic

Objective   Describe the effect on national income when scheduled saving shifts upward and scheduled investment remains constant. Samuelson pages 236-236 and Figure 31-2 on page 236

Pretest Answer   Green, D

Notes (Content reminders, visuals, exercises, activities)

Enabling Questions

Figure 3.2

H.S. 304	CARD #2

ECONOMICS

SUGGESTED % 85

Assignment   5   THEORY OF NATIONAL INCOME DE-
TERMINATION (CONCLUDED)

Topic   Investment and Income

Subtopic

Objective   Distinguish between "autonomous" investment
and "induced" investment. Samuelson page 237

Pretest Answer   Yellow, A

Notes

Enabling Question

Figure 3.3

HS 304   CARD # 3
ECONOMICS

SUGGESTED % 85

Assignment   5   THEORY OF NATIONAL INCOME DE-
TERMINATION (CONCLUDED)
Topic   Investment and Income
Subtopic
Objective   Define the term "paradox of thrift," and ex-
plain how thriftiness affects national income (a)
at a depressed level and (b) at an inflated level.
Samuelson pages 237-239
Pretest Answer   (a) Orange, B
(b) Blue, C

Notes

Enabling Questions

Figure 3.4

HS 304   Card # 4
ECONOMICS

                                              SUGGESTED % 85

Assignment   5   THEORY OF NATIONAL INCOME DE-
                    TERMINATION (CONCLUDED)
Topic   Deflationary and Inflationary
                    Gaps
Subtopic
Objective   Define the term "deflationary gap," and ex-
                    plain how a deflationary gap affects income.
                    Samuelson pages 240-241
Pretest Answer   Green, D

Notes

Enabling Question

Figure 3.5

HS 304	CARD # 5
ECONOMICS	
	SUGGESTED % 85

Assignment	5 THEORY OF NATIONAL INCOME DE-TERMINATION (CONCLUDED)
Topic	Deflationary and Inflationary Gaps
Subtopic	
Objective	Define the term "inflationary gap." Samuelson pages 241-242
Pretest Answer	Green, D

Notes

Enabling Question

Figure 3.6

HS 304 ECONOMICS	CARD # 6
	SUGGESTED % 90

Assignment	5 THEORY OF NATIONAL INCOME DE- TERMINATION (CONCLUDED)
Topic	Deflationary and Inflationary Gaps
Subtopic	
Objective	Explain how deflationary and inflationary gaps are measured. Samuelson pages 240-241
Pretest Answer	Blue, C

Notes

Engabling Question

Figure 3.7

HS 304
ECONOMICS

CARD # 7

SUGGESTED % 85

Assignment   5   THEORY OF NATIONAL INCOME DE-
              TERMINATION (CONCLUDED)

Topic   Deflationary and Inflationary
              Gaps

Subtopic

Objective   Using 45-degree line diagrams, illustrate (a) a
              deflationary gap, and (b) an inflationary gap.
              Samuelson pages 240-241 and Figures 13-5 and
              13-6 on pages 240 and 241

Pretest Answer Green, D

Notes

Enabling Question

Figure 3.8

HS 304	CARD # 8
ECONOMICS	SUGGESTED % 90

Assignment	5 THEORY OF NATIONAL INCOME DE-TERMINATION (CONCLUDED)
Topic	Deflationary and Inflationary Gaps
Subtopic	
Objective	Explain the term "demand-pull inflation." Samuelson pages 241-242
Pretest Answer	Black, E

Notes

Enabling Question

Figure 3.9

HS 304 ECONOMICS	CARD # 9
	SUGGESTED % 85

Assignment 5 THEORY OF NATIONAL INCOME DE-
TERMINATION (CONCLUDED)

Topic Fiscal Policy

Subtopic

Objective Define the term "fiscal policy," and explain the
purpose for which it is used. Samuelson page
243

Pretest Answer Orange, B

Notes

Enabling Question

Figure 3.10

HS 304   CARD # 10
ECONOMICS

                                                    SUGGESTED % 85

Assignment   5   THEORY OF NATIONAL INCOME DE-
                        TERMINATION (CONCLUDED)
Topic   Fiscal Policy
Subtopic
Objective   Given a 45-degree line diagram, explain the
                    change in equilibrium when "G" is added to
                    "C" and "I." Samuelson page 243 and Figure
                    13-7 on page 243
Pretest Answer   Green, D

Notes

Enabling Question
   1. What does "G" represent?
   2. What does the sum "C+I+G" represent?
   3. What is a "Multiplier"?

Figure 3.11

HS 304	CARD # 11
ECONOMICS	
	SUGGESTED % 90

Assignment	5 THEORY OF NATIONAL INCOME DE-TERMINATION (CONCLUDED)
Topic	Fiscal Policy
Subtopic	
Objective	Assuming that all other factors remain constant, (a) explain the effect on national income of an increase in government expenditure, and (b) explain the effect on both national and disposable income of an increase or decrease in taxes.
Pretest Answer	(a) Orange, B
	(b) Yellow, A

Notes

Enabling Question

Figure 3.12

HS 304	CARD # 12
ECONOMICS	
	SUGGESTED % 90

Assignment   5   THEORY OF NATIONAL INCOME DE-
TERMINATION (CONCLUDED)

Topic   Fiscal Policy

Subtopic

Objective   Given the necessary information, calculate the increase in personal income tax required to reduce the inflationary gap. Samuelson pages 244-245

Pretest Answer   Black, E

Notes

Enabling Question

Figure 3.13

HS 304	CARD # 13
ECONOMICS	SUGGESTED % 90

Assignment	5 THEORY OF NATIONAL INCOME DE-TERMINATION (CONCLUDED)
Topic	Fiscal Policy
Subtopic	
Objective	Given the necessary information, calculate the change in national income that would result from a concurrent increase in both taxes and government expenditures. Samuelson pages 244-245 and Assignment 5 Objective 11
Pretest Answer	Orange, B

Notes

Enabling Question

Figure 4

HS 304   ASSIGNMENT 5
ECONOMICS

THEORY OF NATIONAL INCOME DETERMINATION
(CONCLUDED)

Card#   **CONTENT OUTLINE**

1. Investment and income

1   a. How shifts in the consumption schedule affect
              income

②   b. The difference between autonomous and induced
              investment

3   c. The paradox of thrift

④, ⑤   2. Deflationary and inflationary gaps

6, 7   a. Measurement of deflationary and inflationary gaps

⑧   b. Demand-pull inflation

9   3. Fiscal policy in income determination

⑩,11   a. Government spending policies

12,⑬   b. Government tax policies

Danny G. Langdon is the Director of Instructional Design Research, The American College, Bryn Mawr, Pa. In his current capacity, Mr. Langdon conducts research to find more effective and efficient approaches to student learning. He has innovated several new approaches to learning, and is the founder of the *Zimdex* audio indexing system. Formerly a chemistry teacher in the U.S. Peace Corps and public, secondary education in the U.S.A., Mr. Langdon gained much of his experience in developing and researching instructional programs in education and business through his work at General Programmed Teaching, Inc., Palo Alto, California, and the Parks Job Corps Center, Pleasanton, California. Mr. Langdon has contributed several articles and a book, plus conducted workshops in the general field of Instructional Technology.